MKLM Library

WHOSE EXPERIENCE
COUNTS
IN THEOLOGICAL
REFLECTION?

The 1982 Pere Marquette
Theology Lecture

WHOSE EXPERIENCE COUNTS IN THEOLOGICAL REFLECTION?

by

MONIKA HELLWIG

Professor of Theology
Georgetown University

MARQUETTE UNIVERSITY PRESS
MILWAUKEE, WISCONSIN 53233

Library of Congress Catalog Number 82-80331
ISBN 0-87462-537-8

Preface

The 1982 Pere Marquette Lecture, thirteenth in a series since the Tercentenary Celebration of the missions and explorations of Père Jacques Marquette, S.J. (1637-1675). The Marquette University Theology Department, founded in 1952, launched these annual lectures by distinguished theologians under the title of the Pere Marquette Lectures in 1969.

The 1982 lecture was delivered at Marquette University on April 18, 1982, by Dr. Monika Hellwig, theology professor at Georgetown University, lecturer and author of numerous books on faith and theology. Her latest book, *Understanding Catholicism,* (1981) examines the role in theology of the faith-experience of neglected minorities within the Church, such as women and blacks, and of others (the non-specialist, the poor and the oppressed) whose experience remains unexpressed or unexpressible in official theology.

Monika Hellwig was born in Germany (Breslau), educated in England (Liverpool) and in the United States. She holds a Master's Degree and a Doctorate in theology from Catholic University. She has taught at Georgetown since 1967. Her works include *What are the Theologians Saying?*, *The Meaning of the Sacraments*, *The Eucharist and the Hunger of the World*, *What Are They Saying About Death and Hope?*, and others.

Whose Experience Counts in Theological Reflection?

This series honors the memory of an intrepid explorer of this continent with essays concerning explorations of a different kind. The apostolic zeal that led Père Marquette to embark on his risky canoe trips into utterly uncharted waterways speaks eloquently to our own situation. Zeal for the reign of God in our times seems to call for some risky expeditions into reaches of human experience yet unexplored by conventional theology. The event that we have cause to remember with admiration and gratitude three centuries later involved five men in two canoes. That also seems curiously apt for out times, for the explorations into human experience which are so urgently called for in theology today are for the most part quite humble and simple and immediate, without vast master plans, elaborate resources or paralyzing technical equipment.

Two years ago, in this series, Father Frederick Crowe discussed the work of Ber-

nard Lonergan in this connection.[1] He
pointed out that Father Lonergan envisages a shift in thinking as radical as those
which occurred through the work of Aris-
totle and of Francis Bacon. That shift
would effect a profound transformation
and a new beginning in theology because
the shift is relevant whenever people are
studying the past of a tradition or community in order that the wisdom of the past
may guide them into and through the
future.[2] The shift that Lonergan envisages
concerns the effective and comprehensive
collaboration of eight necessary specializa-
tions which have their own methods and
conditions. These are: the competent retrieval of data, their interpretation, their
viewing as part of the larger history, and
their critical evaluation, all as part of the
analytic task; then, as parts of the constructive task, the grounding of the whole endeavor in its human and Christian foundations (involving intellectual, moral and
religious conversions), leading forward to
the fresh formulation of doctrine, its inte-
gration in systematic exposition and its
communication.[3]

Besides demonstrating the urgency of

extensive and patient teamwork in theology today, Lonergan's scheme addresses the problem of religious plurality and of unbelief in the ranks of the scholars necessarily involved in such team work.[4] According to his scheme, the participation of the "unconverted" in the four phases of the analytic task is relatively unproblematic. It is in the four phases of the constructive task that the depth of conversion, intellectual, moral and religious, begins to play a decisive role. More especially, the whole work hinges on the authenticity of the foundations; its whole value is critically at risk in the grounding of the endeavor in its human and Christian reality. This poses a challenge of considerable force and complexity to theological investigation undertaken in the context of the contemporary university with its criteria for hiring, firing and promotion, its AAUP guidelines and its legal constraints.

In spite of these difficulties and constraints, the Lonergan scheme does describe the transformation that is in fact already going on in professional theology in its more conventional settings. A move on the one hand towards greater technical

competence through more comprehensive
use of related disciplines is converging with
a thrust on the other hand towards what A.
J. Heschel was wont to call "depth
theology" on the analogy of depth psycho-
logy,[5] Yet there is a groundswell of prophe-
tic protest among the communities of
Christians, and here and there even among
the ranks of professional theologians, concerning a further, perhaps more radical
transformation needed in the process of doing theology.

This protest is focussed on what Lonergan calls "foundations". It is related to the
distinction observed by Karl Rahner in
current Christologies between ascending
and descending approaches, those that
begin with dogmatic affirmations and those
that begin with experience, observation
and reflection upon these.[6] From many
quarters today, the protest sounds forth
that theology ought to be based upon experience. In some sense, of course, this has
always been acknowledged. Thus, for instance, John Macquarrie, intending simply
to present the traditional understanding of
the task of theology, names the formative
factors in theology as six: experience, reve-

lation, scripture, tradition, culture and reason.[7] Macquarrie puts experience first on his list because "theology implies participation in a religious faith, so that some experience of the life of faith precedes theology and may indeed be said to motivate it...and the process of bringing the faith-experience to clear expression in words embarks us on the business of theology".[8]

This much is generally agreed, but it seems that the question being raised in so many quarters today, whether wonderingly, hesitantly, petulantly, confidently or with discouragement, is the question, "*whose* faith experience"? If one moves through the task of theology according to the sequence of the eight specialties as delineated by Lonergan, there is a difficulty. This difficulty is not particular to Lonergan but pervasive in conventional professional theology. Lonergan's analysis simply serves to make it explicit. According to that scheme the theological task begins with the retrieval of data from the earlier phases of the tradition and moves, by way of interpretation, historical perspective and evaluation, towards the constructive phase in which the theologian grounds his or her

understanding in the foundations of his or
her human and Christian experience, in
order to formulate doctrines appropriately
and integrate them in a system which can
be communicated.

There is no doubt that such a movement from past to present is *an* inevitable
task of a theology that claims to be Christian (as it would be indeed of a theology
that claimed to be Jewish or Muslim).
What is not clear is that this scheme has
any right to claim to be *the* task of theology,
nor even that it rightfully claims the central
position. I believe it is this claim which is
being challenged so widely today and that
that is what constitutes the real revolution
in Christian theology.

The reason for the challenge, I think, is
that while experience is honored in the
scheme it is the experience of the past
rather than the present. Moreover, when at
the point of the "foundations" the experience of the present is brought to bear on
the project, that experience is necessarily
that of the professional theologian. It is
envisaged of course that it is the experience
of the professional theologian as believer. It
is even explicitly acknowledged, both by

Lonergan in his exposition[9] and by theologians generally in their manner of proceeding, that the experience must be that of the theologian as member of a believing community bringing the experience of that community to expression. Yet the scrutiny of what might be significant to express is always being made from more or less the same human bias — heavily male, largely celibate, usually clerical, economically privileged (that is, very seldom really poor, hungry, despised, bullied and frightened), almost always educated in certain fairly narrowly defined traditions of literature, science, philosophy and notions of what constitutes scholarly pursuit of truth, very generally by temperament and disposition introverted and more attracted to the further reaches of abstraction than to the exigences of structuring human life in society and coping with its inevitable problems.

It is of course true that some aspects of the bias can be cured and that a present trend in that direction is discernible with lay and female, married and parenting, third world and persecuted and even activist theologians. Yet all of these continue to be marginal and while they have been most

vocal and most articulately literary in their
protest, it is clear that the problem is not
only nor even primarily in the persons who
occupy the slots, but rather in the way the
task is understood. If the essential, or central, or only task of theology is to move
from a complex and highly technical, time-
consuming, linguistically, historically and
philosophically skilled, grasp of the past
development and deposits of the tradition,
into the confronting of present questions,
then it is assured that only a certain type of
person can set out on the enterprise, and
that that person is going to continue (in
spite of all efforts to the contrary) to look
more or less like the persons described
above.

It is for this reason, I believe, that there
is a shift in theology that seems to be more
radical than that envisaged by Lonergan in
Method in Theology and which is already
causing earthquakes in the churches. It
might be viewed, however, in relation to
the spiralling pattern in the development of
dogma which was suggested by Lonergan
much earlier[10], that is, the spiral that
moves through "trans-cultural", theological
and dogmatic change involving polarity

and tension. The present trend, not without much conflict and bewilderment, seems to be towards a contrapuntal perception of theology — simultaneous processes of ascending and descending theologies that need to be combined in such a way that one does not simply subsume and dominate the other. There is a movement from present experience to reflection and evaluation first in existential terms and then by correlation with the tradition and its established formulations.[11] This movement claims to be theology properly speaking on an equal footing with the theology that proceeds from the tradition in order to explain it in present categories.

This has, of course, been maintained for some time by professional theologians such as Karl Rahner with his combination of transcendental and historical approaches, and Paul Tillich with his acknowleged existentialist presuppositions and method of correlation. However, the shift went considerable further in the political theology of J. B. Metz, in the liberation theology coming from the Third World, in black theology, in further and as yet unsubstantiated claims for other ethnic theologies, in the thrust for feminine theology, in the claims for the hermeneutic privilege of the poor and the oppressed, and not least in the ubiquitous phenomenon of action/reflection groups in which Christians engaged in social ministries or in experiments with more exigent forms of community explicitly claim to do theological reflection grounded and validated in the first place in their present and unique experience.

In all of these cases, the explicit or implicit argument is that the relationship between the non-specialists reflecting on their own Christian experience and the specialist bringing testimonies out of the tradition to contemporary formulation is not the relationship of the inexpert to the expert, nor that of those who have questions to one who can answer them, nor of people with problems to a person who can solve them, nor even of those who bring their experience to one who can interpret it for them. The contention is that there is a reciprocity and exchange of functions in which both sides bring experience and both sides are interpreters, both sides come with questions and both sides offer answers, both have problems and both solve them. Both, therefore, have expertise to offer, and this seems to be part of a general movement away from exaggerated or exclusive reliance upon certain professional experts in various fields.

There seem to be two major strands in this development. One of these follows from the existential and transcendentalist positions, moving into political theology and the theological reflection of the charismatic groups and of the *communidades de base* (or basic communities) as well as that of ministry teams and social action groups of various kinds. The emphasis in this strand appears to be the recovery of experience, present experience, community experience, Christian experience, as an acknowledged factor in theology, indeed as foundational. The other strand, following from the same positions, leads to black theology, women's theology, and what is projected in the claims for an hermeneutic privilege of the poor and the oppressed. In this strand the concern is not so much to reinstate the role of experience as to correct a bias in the experience which plays a foundational role in theology. The liberation theology of the

third world, and predominantly of Latin
America, seems to bring together the two
strands, emphasizing on the one hand the
recovery of present experience in its full
social and political dimensions as integral
and foundational in theology, and claiming
on the other hand that the vantage point in
experience from which a truly Christian
perspective emerges is that of the poor, the
marginated, the oppressed.

It should be noted that none of these
positions claim that there is such a thing in
practice as pure experience unshaped and
uninfluenced by theory or tradition. What
is at stake is rather the centrality of the present experience in all its complexity as the
starting point and the continuing reference
point in the theological process. In a more
technical vein, there has been considerable
discussion and analysis of the "hermeneutic
circle" by which perception and appropria-
tion of the classic testimonies is conditioned
and filtered by present experience and the
expectations to which present experience
gives rise, and also *vice versa*. [12] The issue is
not the denial of that hermeneutic circle
but the various ways of understanding it
and of acknowledging it in practice. To

make this more concrete, it will be useful to give examples from some of the positions cited.

As is well known, Karl Rahner's method in theology, which has largely transformed what is possible in Catholic theology and what can be recognized as orthodox in Catholic theology, demands a transcendental analysis of any given question prior to an historical inquiry into the answers given in the tradition.[13] That is to say, there must first be a consideration of what that question can mean in terms of human consciousness, the conditions and possibilities of human knowing, the dimensions of human existence and experience. In other words there will be a consideration that anticipates in some sense what kinds of answers might be given to the question, before searching for the meaning of the answers that have in fact been given. This approach is grounded in an understanding of the role of the human consciousness in creation and history and revelation and in an understanding of essential continuity between creation and redemption, nature and grace. The human person as hearer of God's word is taken in this approach as the

place of revelation, and ordinary human
experience is dignified with a certain im-
mediacy in the relationship with God. In
this understanding the openness to God
revealing Himself, the sincerity and whole-
heartedness of the guest, condition the pos-
sibility of true answers to theological questions. Such questions are not pursued by
logic alone.

In the thought of J. B. Metz, there is
substantial agreement with this stance of
Rahner. But Metz finds Rahner's pursuit
of his method too individualistic, introspective and a-historical. For Metz the problem
of fundamental theology (which is his field)
is not primarily a matter of reconciling past
statements with present understanding nor
even of reflecting upon present individual
experience and bringing it into dialog with
the legacy from the past. It is rather the
task of asking whether in the present political, social and economic situation of the
human race, (a situation which shapes the
conditions of being and becoming for the
individuals within it), the gospel has any
further meaning at all and is indeed good
news.[14] That means that not only the individual experience but the public and social

experience, that of constructing and maintaining political and economic structures, that of conflicts of interests and wars and class struggles, is to be taken seriously as grounding theological reflection, understanding and formulation.

The assumption underlying this is that God reveals Himself and is creatively and redemptively at work in the totality of human life in the world, that there is no properly profane sphere. Theological reflection, therefore, is properly drawn from the social and political action of Christians and their experiences of organizational responsibility and transformations. Theology is political not because it can be applied to political situations once the theological principles are clearly determined and the dogmatic formulations are in place, nor because it touches upon the political at its periphery, but rather because the central questions upon which a theology must be built rise out of our human life together confronting the challenge of human destiny. This, then, gives key significance to the so-called secular sphere of experience which is the arena of public affairs and social accountability. It claims, in effect,

that there is an inexorable demand for salvation arising out of the whole social situation that must be heard and examined in its
own right in order to understand what God
promises and demands and does in the
world, because such understanding can not
simply be superimposed from preconceived
theological categories drawn from academic studies of the past.

Contrary to what may first appear,
much of the theological reflection that
arises out of charismatic groups and basic
communities seems to be a kind of political
theology writ small. At least it is reflection
on social interaction and responsibility on a
small scale within the groups which are trying to structure their relationships and
social configurations by the Spirit of Jesus
and the anticipation by faith, hope and
charity of the rule of God. They too theologize on the basis of their own experience of
what really happens in the structures of
society, in the intractable patterns as well
as in the transformations, in those things
that are destructive and come to be recognized as grace. Although they are dealing
with the social situation on a small scale,
and more particularly with the social situa-

tion deliberately taken as Christian responsibility by fervent believers, they also are obstinately convinced that God reveals Himself in this ongoing social situation and that they can not simply superimpose preconceived categories in order to understand what salvation means and to recognize what is the work of God among them. Such understanding and recognition are understood to come from the progressive conversion not only of individuals but of the group, and such group conversion is necessarily a conversion of structures. It is at this juncture that their mode of theological reflection appears as a small scale exercise of political theology.[15]

Even more obviously in the line of a political theology is the theological reflection that emerges from a variety of action groups for social justice, for peace, for slum clearance and better housing for the city poor and so forth.[16] Implicit in the reflection of these groups on their experiences is the understanding that sin is revealed in suffering. The patter of original sin and general sinfulness and need of redemption are revealed in the social and political structures that cause suffering on a large scale. By a process of negation of such suffering and therefore of the structures that cause it, human hope begins to acquire shape and content. That negation can be purely speculative or it can be practical and experiential for those giving shape to the hope. That is to say, scholars and professional analysts can, of course, construct theoretical models for the solution of particular kinds of social suffering. As we all know, such theoretical models again and again fail to reckon with human freedom, sin and selfishness, lethargy, the factor of trust and the real motivations underlying the variety of human responses. When, on the other hand, the projection of solutions and the shaping of hope spring from immediate, generous, constructive but often heartbreaking involvement in the problems and their solution, there is a certain resilience and realism in the expectations and in the understanding of the situation.

Reasonably enough, those who are involved practically in action for social justice or peace are often reluctant to listen to "experts" whose expertise consists of knowledge of the past and of the theory, as though knowledge of the present and of the practice were to be reckoned as the position of the inexpert. Christians involved in such action come to it with some initial understanding of their faith and its scriptures and tradition. But from their interaction with the situation of sin and suffering they are constantly adjusting and refining that understanding. From their deepening experience they return to the scriptures and the tradition asking what they have to say by way of revealing God's purpose and promise and present healing in the midst of suffering and struggle and confusion. What is important, however, is that in asking these questions of scripture and tradition, such practically involved Christians in our times are not asking the scholars or the Church *magisterium* for answers to their questions. At most they are asking for some technical assistance in the finding and the correct reading of the sources. Sometimes they are not even asking for this, because they perceive that the technical apparatus has been elaborated without reference to faith or commitment, possibly to the point of obscuring the faith content.

The attitude in this is not one of anti-intellectualism. It is based on an under-

standing of what it is that constitutes wisdom and knowledge, on an understanding
more particularly of what constitutes theology. Theology, as the systematic reflection
on what we can learn of God and of God's
dealings with us, is focussed for Christians
on the person of Jesus as the central point
of revelation. This much is agreed. It is a
question, however, of the ways in which
Christians approach the revelatory person
and message of Jesus in order to see what
he reveals. The approach in much of what
the action reflection groups are doing is one
not so much of looking *at* Jesus through the
testimonies of those closer to his times, but
one of looking *with* Jesus through the acti-
vities of caring about people and situations
concerning which he cared. It is not so
much a matter of trying to discern what
Jesus did in the world as the Word of God,
but of trying to see what Jesus the truly
human saw the transcendent Father doing
in the world creatively and redemptively.

The purpose of the quest is not to find
out what Jesus did by way of response and
copy it. It seems that it is not even to speculate what Jesus would have done in present
circumstances and then to go ahead and do

it. Rather it is to learn to recognize the voice of the Father, of the transcendent God, speaking to us today in our experience, that is in our total experience in the human community with all its complexity. This is why the answer to the question is not to be found in books, not even the Bible, nor in the voices of human authorities, whether they be those of scholars or of the Church *magisterium*. Texts and authorities can at most be helpful in acquiring sense and discrimination for the voice of God in present experience. In such a view, theology is never the logical extrapolation of new answers to new questions from the old answers to the old questions. Theology is always systematic reflection on God revealing himself. It always has its home base in what Lonergan calls "foundations".

Two crucial positions are really assumed in this whole understanding of the task of theology: suffering is only really known for what it is by those who suffer, and the self-revelation of God is really only known for what it is by those who are open to receive it in faith and in their personal and community life-style. This leads to what has been referred to above as the second

strand of the current development in theology, namely the dogged insistence that
comes simultaneously from so many quarters that there are distortions to correct in
the conventional ways in which theology
has been done.

That the self-revelation of God is really
only known by those who are open to
receive it in faith is something that has not
theoretically been in dispute. Yet the
reduction of revelation to propositional
truths has for centuries been a tendency in
Christian theology (whether admitted or
not). Such a tendency subtly gives the im-
pression that once these "truths of revelation" have been established, it is simply a
matter of reasoning logically and comprehensively from them. In other words, in
practice faith and commitment, as actualiz-
ed in personal and community life-styles,
are understood to make no effective difference in the theological reflection or conclusions. This is what is being put in question by so many of these groups today.
They claim that faith, commitment and
life-style do make a crucial difference to the
questions that are asked, the way the
answers are sought and tested, and to the

kinds of answers that are found to be satisfactory.

A case in point here is the fundamental eschatological question: what is the content of Christian hope? One can simply answer from the established accounts of the faith, that the content of Christian hope is God himself as end and purpose, reward and fulfillment of human lives. One might amplify that by saying that the content of hope is fullest possible union with God giving greatest possible peace, joy and fulfillment of all longings. One might then further speculate on whether such union is essentially and primarily a matter of the mind or of the will and on what else might be inferred about the nature of such union. To test the answers, one might turn back to the scriptures and the classic and official statements of the tradition to see whether these can be reconciled with the conclusions reached speculatively.

Meanwhile, however, these answers are neither attractive nor pertinent to most human beings. The question people ask in our time are: can we survive the nuclear arms race? will the rich continue to grow richer and the poor poorer until the fabric of society falls apart altogether? is it really written as inevitable in our human destiny that in the midst of ample resurces there will always be vast numbers of people in direst need? must the cities of the whole modern world eventually crumble into violence and be controlled by street gangs and unutterable terror? how can we, as individuals, remain sane under the increasing pressures of a fast-moving society in which contacts, work, living conditions, demands and rewards are more and more impersonal? can we hope for peace and conflict resolution by diplomacy? can we ever hope to repair the appalling racial conflicts and inequities which we have inherited? does everyone have a right to personal dignity, a livelihood, a family and home, the pursuit of happiness, the enjoyment of leisure and beauty, or are these good things necessarily only for the fortunate few? Such are the questions that people are asking. They are, in the last analysis, not secular questions, but questions about the nature of God and the meaning and purpose of God's dealings with us as creatures as well as being questions about our vocation, task and expectation as self-determining creatures, free but dependent and interdependent.

In many different ways the action/reflection groups come from their experience of attempting a deeper Christian community life and from their experiences of working to solve particular social justice problems, and they experience these questions as theological ones in a new and vivid way. They do not perceive them as questions which must be asked in order to make sure of the orthodoxy of one's faith, but rather as questions that must be asked in order to cope with the immediate exigences of ordinary secular life. They have become real and practical questions; they have become questions about life here and now, and yet they are understood as constituting together the basic eschatological question: what is the content of Christian hope?

In attempting to answer such a question, these groups do not turn first to scripture and tradition for authoritative statement which they will then apply. They turn first to their own Christian experience which they seek to interpret in order to discern what it is that God reveals in that experience. Such revelation will be seen both positively and negatively in the experience. That is to say it is read negatively in

suffering, disunity, distrust and a sense of
boredom and lack of goals, and it is read
positively in the moments of joy, reconci-
liation, community, courage, peace and
sense of purpose. What can be is read in
momentary glimpses of what already is in
part. What must be is read in agonizing
experiences that cry out to be changed. In
both cases the gospel as passed on from the
earliest Christian generations and the tradition in its many formulations are read
and interpreted in the light of this present
experience. These people are aware of the
Risen Christ as alive and acting in the community that is Church today. They are
aware of themselves as being at the source
of the tradition in a way not wholly discon-
tinuous from that of the earliest
Christians.[17]

What is significant here is not that such
groups scrutinize others and reject their
theology as ungrounded in deep Christian
faith and radical Christian life styles. Very
little of that seems to occur. The significance of the groundswell in these movements seems to be rather that they scrutinize themselves, both individually and as
communities, in terms of the practical exi-

gences placed on them as Christians in their social and personal contexts, and that they theologize with continuing reflexive awareness of their foundations. They are producing a kind of experimental theology with built-in patterns of reality testing. When they speak of salvation and of the content of hope they do so in the light of their community efforts to respond radically to the good news of salvation and in the light of the experience and insight that results as they reflect on the outcomes of such response. It may well be argued that, after all, academic theologians are not scoundrels or indifferent to their Christian vocation and that they too are surely speaking from foundations of personal faith and Christian commitment of life-style. There is no intent here to deny this. The intent is only to point out the significance of the current movements that put such foundation at the center of reflexive awareness and do so in community groupings.

This foundation in faith and Christian life-style is one crucial assumption in the contemporary revolution in the location and manner of contemporary theological reflection. The other crucial assumption,

which is perhaps more explosive in its con-
sequences, is the understanding that suffering is only really known for what it is by
those who suffer. This applies, of course,
directly to the thrust and claims involved in
black theology, women's theology, liberation theology of all kinds and Third World
theology generally. This is explosive
because Christian theology is necessarily a
theology of redemption from an alienated
and sinful condition, and because it is
suffering which manifests sin and aliena-
tion. If suffering is really only known for
what it is by those who suffer, then it is they
who have privileged access to the understanding of sin and thereby to the message
of salvation from the sinful and alienated
condition. In a general sense one may
speak of the claim that there is an "hermeneutic privilege of the oppressed". [18]

This claim of an "hermeneutic privilege" seems to be most vigorously resisted
by conventional academic theologians in
each situation in which it has been made.
Historically it seems to grow out of the
positions sketched above, that is, those of
Tillich, Rahner, Metz, emphasizing foundations in human experience, and those of

the action/reflection groups which make those foundations practical, communal and political in an immediate sense. It was only to be expected that once present experience was allowed to move into a central position in the process of theology, groups would arise who would raise the question "whose experience?" and would claim to correct a bias in the selection of contemporary experience. The women's movement has done this quite explicitly, and was able to document its case most clearly. Theology for centuries was written, taught, studied and applied in preaching by men. Moreover, for centuries theology was, at least in Roman Catholic circles, largely a matter of explicating and elaborating into a system official Church doctrines which were themselves the formulations of men. Besides, in Roman Catholic circles, for centuries all men involved, or almost all, were celibate and living and working in rather well insulated situations far away from family and other ordinary socio-economic and cultural-political settings. It was not difficult to demonstrate that this represented a very small segment of human and Christian experience, and there has in fact been a grow-

ing concern at least on this side of the
Atlantic to involve women and family people in the process of theology.

What has been interesting, however, is
a certain subtle tension that has emerged.
As in other well-established professions,
women have been allowed or even invited
into academic and professional theology
with the understanding that the proper and
respectable way to do it has already been
established and that the newcomers will do
it the way that it is done. They come in, so
to speak, as the apprentices of those who
are already there and learn the assumptions and methods from them. Indeed they
learn the prejudices that are built into the
assumptions and methods because people
are not aware of their own prejudices and
can not distinguish them from knowledge
and wisdom unless and until challenged by
someone who sees the situation from a
different vantage point. This is to some ex-
tent an inevitable process. But eventually
the apprentices become not only journey-
men but masters. If the emphasis in their
training has been on tradition, they are
more than likely to continue to press the
claims of the established patterns. But this

has not been the case for theologians trained in the last several decades. Rather there
has already been a strong emphasis on
experience in the leading theological positions taught during this time. Eventually
these new masters are likely to assert their
own experience in more original and creative ways.

This seems to be more or less what has
happened, and I believe that the Christian
community at large and the theological
profession in particular were not unpre-
pared for it, though some may have been
startled by the vehemence and stridency
with which the experience of women has
been asserted in theology.[19] However, the
assertion of women's experience does not
really stop with the claim to correct an
existing bias. It contains more than a suggestion that the women's movement is
essentially linked with movements for black
liberation and for the liberation of all oppressed groups by the key factor that it is
those who suffer from injustice, oppression,
deprivation or exclusion who have privileged access to an understanding of what
is wrong with the situation and to the dis-
cernment of the true message of hope and

salvation from that situation. It would, I think, be readily granted that each of these represents only one kind of suffering among many that point to the need of redemption, but these particular kinds of social suffering are seen as paradigmatic for the whole human situation.

What appears to have been relatively easy for women to demonstrate has been more problematic for black theologians speaking and writing on behalf of the black situation in North America in particular and in the world in general. It has not been so immediately apparent that racial exclusion of sectors of human experience was a significant distortion in Christian theology. Black Americans and other oppressed peoples have striven with some difficulty to make the dominant peoples of the world aware that the dominated peoples not only had a very different experience of human existence in human society with all its ills and injustices, but also had powerful and paradigmatic experiences of the savior God in the sinful and tragic patterns of human history. They brought a whole new understanding to the Exodus theme as appropriated by the followers of Jesus[20]. They also brought a whole new understanding of Jesus as representative of the systematically and racially oppressed[21] and in this added considerable depth to the understanding of the redemption. It is a depth to which the conventional soteriology did not really penetrate, yet which those of us who are not so oppressed can recognize once it is brought to our attention.[22]

The way that has been opened up by black theology has been pursued further by some authors who attempt to formulate a theology of, for and by the oppressed and who claim either for the poor in material resources or for the oppressed generally a privileged access to the self-revelation of the savior God in history and a privileged access, therefore, to the meaning of the Christian gospel of salvation.[23] This widened scope of the claim has appeared as the most controversial of all. While women and black theologians, as well as the theologians of the Third World have spoken for themselves and spoken for an experience that was their own, those who claim an "hermeneutic privilege" for the materially poor as such are seldom themselves really poor. Though occasionally they are poor

by choice, this is a different base of experience. Therefore these people have really
made themselves a channel to speak for the
experience of others, and what they are
saying is already at one step removed from
the experience itself. [24]

However, it is not only because the
position is being proposed by people who
speak for others and not for themselves that
it has caused so much antagonism. It is
rather, I believe, because this claim on
behalf of the poor, oppressed and dispos-
sessed as such raises the question of expertise in its most acute form. Such people are
generally unlearned, for the most part un-
cultured. They are not trained to critical
reflection, nor widely read. They have not
been taught to think in abstractions, they
have not been schooled to "objectivity", nor
are they usually thoughtfully and exigently
introspective. We do not usually expect
them to offer creative solutions to problems. To claim for them an "hermeneutic
privilege" is to value something other than
intellectual acuity, good information, and
scholarly competence in the interpretation
of God's self-revelation in history. Therefore it moves us away from the sphere of

our accustomed certitudes and probabili-
ties, from the criteria with which we are at
ease, from rational and detached demon-
stration, from readily verifiable standards
of reliability. It moves us into the realm in
which verification can only be out of our
own experience, in which, therefore, experience of sinfulness, vulnerability, reconci-
liation, community, must be acknowledged
in our own lives affectively as well as intel-
lectually in order to become the touchstone
of truth in our perceptions of God's dealings with us. It moves us closer to a biblical
sense of truth as that which is firm and can
be relied upon in the contingencies of life
and in the wagers that we make with our
freedom. We have been accustomed to a
notion of theology as an academic pursuit
conducted on a purely intellectual basis
and safely removed from the perilous realm
of affectivity and historical contingency.
The claim on behalf of the truly poor chal-
lenges this rather ruthlessly.

There is a further reason for deep distrust and excessively vehement reactions
against any suggestion of an "hermeneuti-
cal privilege" of the poor. If the category of
the poor is taken in its most basic sense of

the materially deprived who are usually
also culturally deprived, ignorant, inarticulate and uncouth, if it is taken to include
the urban poor of the ghetto, the migrant
poor, the displaced, the unemployed, we
are not dealing with an idyllic portrait. We
are speaking of people who are often feck-
less and irresponsible, among whom the
crime rate is very high especially in inci-
dents of outright violence, who tend to be
lazy and dirty and insolent. In other words,
we are speaking of people who do not ex-
emplify what we normally take to be basic
and necessary virtues. Moreover, we usually assume that those who succeed are
those who deserve to succeed, upon whom
God's favor rests, and who must therefore
understand God's dealings better than
those who find themselves outside this
realm of manifest election. The notion
that, according to the biblical vision of reality, God's predilection is for the poor because of their poverty, is in itself one that
we tend to resist. That God favors people
not for their achievements in virtue or
other endeavors but for their simple need,
is already difficult to accept. The problem
is enhanced when we are speaking not only

of God's predilection for the poor, but of their understanding their human situation before God better. It always seems to us that surely those understand it best who are virtuous and have diligently studied.

The claim of an "hermeneutic privilege" of the poor with regard to the gospel of salvation is really a way of stating that actual, ordinary poverty is an effective paradigm for the human situation in which we all find ourselves. If the experience of economic poverty is in some special and immediate way revelatory of the creating and redeeming God, it is surely not because the poor are expecially virtuous but because the poor can not help knowing their poverty and their need. Poverty is insufficiency of personal resources, dependence on others, helplessness. The poor can not so easily mask their sins and inadequacies. Certainly they can not pretend to be sufficient unto themselves. They can not live as though they were invulnerable. They can not assume an inflated importance based on achievement, expertise or virtue. Their relation to God is clearly in their creatureliness and need and their relation to other human persons is in their simple existence and in their shared humanity and interdependence. That is why the paradigm of the human situation according to the Christian understanding is not in the person who is wise or learned or virtuous but in the person who is poor.[25]

The question might still be raised whether the claim of an "hermeneutic privilege" for the experience of poverty exaggerates the advantage. The claim has, of course, also been made in relation to the analysis of the social situation but that is a different problem.[26] In relation to the good news of salvation the case seems to be straightforward enough. The need for redemption is known in the experience of unfreedom, of bondage and oppression, of suffering that is seen not as occasional but as pervasive in the human situation. The poor and oppressed know not only *that* they need redemption but they know also some of the depth and shape and quality of the redemption that they need because it is the depth and shape and quality of their deprivation and suffering and confusion. The rich, of course have suffering and deprivation and confusion in their lives too, but they can more readily "buy" themselves out of it, or at least out of the realization of it. The wise and learned likewise know suffering and deprivation and confusion no less, but they can all too easily reason themselves into denial of it, put it in brackets, focus their attention elsewhere. The poor have fewer defenses, and to be defenseless is surely to be more alert for good news of impending rescue.

The case has been pressed further than this, for it is claimed[27] that Jesus preached the good news to the poor among a subject people under alien domination. The poor, therefore, recognize and interpret the message concretely and directly, while those who are not poor and oppressed encounter the message as mediated through a series of abstractions and reapplications to the concrete. The assumption here is that the poor come with their own experience and find immediate resonance and familiarity in the gospel not because they pray much or study diligently but because it does indeed describe a situation which they recognize without effort.

The question arises as to how we can verify such readier understanding in the poor if we are neither poor nor oppressed

ourselves, for if it can not be verified there
is little purpose in discussing the matter.
But this problem throws us back to the
starting point and, so to speak, begs the
question. If the verification that is sought is
to be according to the accepted procedures
of conventional academic theology, it is
likely to exclude the claim on principle.
This will certainly be so if it is axiomatic
that sound interpretation is based upon
accurate retrieval of data from the past, interpreted in their own historical and cultur-
al setting by the usual academic criteria, set
in their proper developmental sequence
and critically evaluated, leading then to an
establishing of foundations in order to ar-
rive at fresh formulations of doctrine inte-
grated into systematic exposition for later
communication in pastoral situations.[28]

Clearly this expectation can only vali-
date conclusions reached by conventional
theological procedures. To use such expectations in critique and evaluation of theological reflection or conclusions reached by
others than professional theologians is certainly to find oneself ruling these out. In
other words, the rules of the theological
game are set up in such a way that only the

experience of theologians counts in the present, and that only if it can be fitted within a frame of reference constructed out of the experience of the past. The expectations by which such a claim as that for the hermeneutic privilege of the poor can be evaluated must therefore be one which is more than a description of the way academic theology is done. The question then is this: can any such criteria be found?

It is at this point that the mediation of those who speak for the inarticulate poor becomes significant. It is important to ask *why* these articulate persons who are not poor, except perchange by voluntary renunciation and then never really poor in culture, or connections, or life-options, discern authenticity and truth in the understanding that the poor have of God's self-revelation. These are people who have been close enough to the poor, vulnerable enough in empathy with the poor to hear what they are saying in their clumsy and inarticulate ways, and to be personally moved by it. When they express the reasons for their acceptance of that interpretation of God's self-revelation which they have gleaned from the poor, these reasons

seem to be based on something close to
Rahner's transcendental approach, or
Tillich's method of correlation, but most of
all they seem to express what John Henry
Newman named as the "illative sense"[29].
They testify that when they try to divest
themselves of prejudices and enter into the
vision of the poor they experience a har-
mony and coherence which simply "ring
true" in the understanding that they find
there of the saving God and the human
situation before that God. Recognizing the
experience of the poor as paradigmatic
from their own experience brought to more
vivid awareness, they turn then to scripture
and tradition to ask whether they read
coherently from this perspective and find
that indeed they do.

Quite apart from the truth of this particular claim about the hermeneutic privilege of the poor and oppressed, the claim
raises the question of the role of experience
in theological reflection, that is, the interpretation of God's self-revelation in the
human situation in history, and the question of the testing of claims made for experience and of interpretations based on the
experience. The claim raises this question

with reference to a much wider range of current movements in theological reflection. The basic issue under that wider range of theological reflection is: whose experience counts? and how can relevant experience be made to count?

Obviously these questions are far from being answered. However, the liberation theology of Latin America and other sectors of the Third World has made some significant contributions towards an answer. Its representative authors[30] have attempted to hold in balance not only the assertion of present experience against a certain monopoly for the experience of the past, and the correction of the bias against the experience of the poorer and less powerful people, but also the need to take into account technical information about the structures and institutions of society which shape and condition people's experience of life and their very survival or destruction. The liberation theologians have been much criticized, even ridiculed, in conventional theological circles for proclaiming a grandiose project which they are not able to carry out properly. It is true that they are not able to carry it out because the demands are vast and complex. It is, however, also true that this is what must be done if Christian theology is to tackle the questions about hope and salvation and the nature of God which people in the contemporary world are asking with increasing urgency.

The liberation theologians also are asking and answering the question, whose experience counts in theological reflection? They are perhaps answering it more comprehensively than other groups by the way they relate praxis and theory, which brings into the scope of their inquiry in principle the whole sweep of the social sciences and of statistical data retrieval possibilities in the contemporary human experience seen as objectified. This has laid them open, of course, to the objection that the data of theology are found in divine revelation and not in statistical surveys.

This also begs the question of how God reveals himself in history and how that revelation surfaces, so to speak, in our experience. If we may assume that the experience in which God's self-revelation happens is not only in the past but also in the present, not only in special persons but in the human person and community as such, not only in conventionally religious forms but in the course of everyday events, not as a rare and extraordinary moment but as a continuing reality, can we also assume that that divine self-revelation is encountered in complex human social interactions as well as in individualistic perceptions of human experience? There appears to be no good reason to exclude such complex human social interactions and the patterns of human possibilities and human limits that emerge from them when they are studied systematically in the context of the social sciences.

If this is true, then liberation theology also raises questions about the role of experience in theology and about the testing of that experience and of interpretation based upon it, which go beyond the works of the liberation theologians and question the whole project of theology for the future. They question the methods and the sources and the very definition of what is properly theology. Thus the question, *whose* experience counts in theological reflection? turns into a question that is more than methodological, for it addresses the understanding of salvation, revelation and truth. That is why I see this question as the pervasive and truly revolutionary one in contemporary theology, and that is also why I see the theological reflection of groups that are not professional theologians as meriting the most respectful attention both from professional theologians and from the hierarchic Church.

NOTES

1. See *Method in Theology: an Organon for Our Time* by Frederick E. Crowe, S.J., Milwaukee: Marquette University Press, 1980.

2. *Ibid.,* p. 37.

3. See *Method in Theology,* by Bernard J.F. Lonergan, S.J., N.Y.: Herder, 1972, especially pp. 127-133.

4. *Ibid.,* p. 268.

5. See, for instance, *God in Search of Man,* by Abraham Joshua Heschel. N.Y.: Harper & Row, 1966. p. 7.

6. See, "The Two Basic Types of Christology", in *Theological Investigations,* Vol. XIII, by Karl Rahner. N.Y.: Seabury, 1975. pp. 213-223.

7. *Principles of Christian Theology.* N.Y.: Scribners, 1966. p. 4.

8. *Ibid.,* p. 5.

9. *Method,* p. 269.

10. *Cf. De Deo Trino.* Rome: Gregorian University, 1964. Caput I. Sections 7 & 8. pp. 42-53.

11. The term correlation is, of course, taken from Paul Tillich. See, for instance, his *Systematic Theology,* Vol. I. Chicago: University of Chicago Press, 1951. pp. 59-66.

12. See, for instance, *The Liberation of Theology,* by Juan Luis Segundo, S.J., N.Y.: Orbis, 1975. Ch. 1.

13. See *Foundations of Theology,* by Karl Rahner. N.Y.: Seabury, 1978. Introduction, Section 3, pp. 14-23.

14. *Toward a Theology of the World,* by J.B. Metz. N.Y.: Herder, 1969.

15. See, for instance, *The New Community,* by Elizabeth O'Connor. Harper & Row, 1976. See also the publications of the Focolarini.

16. See, for instance, the periodicals, *The Other Side, Sojourners,* and the publications of the Center for Concern in Washington, D.C.

17. *Cf. Doing Theology in New Places.* ed. Jean-Pierre Jossua and J.B. Metz. N.Y.: Seabury, 1979.

18. For a survey of this claim, see "The Hermeneutic Privilege of the Oppressed", by Lee Cormie, in *The Proceedings of the Thirty-Third Annual Convention of the Catholic Theological Society of America,* ed. Luke Salm, FSC. Bronx, N.Y.: CTSA, 1978. pp. 155-181.

19. One might point to the writings of Rosemary Ruether and Mary Daly, for instance.

20. This is particularly so, of course, in the sermons and leadership of Martin Luther King.

21. *Cf. The Black Messiah,* by Albert Cleage. N.Y.: Sheed & Ward, 1968. The theme is proposed in the introduction, but many of the essays contribute to its elucidation.

22. *Cf.,* for instance, what Albert Nola does with the theme in *Jesus before Christianity.* N.Y.: Orbis, 1980.

23. This claim is made especially by Julio de Santa Ana in his book, *Good News to the Poor,* N.Y.: Orbis, 1979, and in a book he edited for the World Council of Churches, *Toward a Church of the Poor.* N.Y.: Orbis, 1979. But see also, for example, *Letters from the Desert,* by Carlo Carretto (a Little Brother of Jesus). N.Y.: Orbis, 1972.

24. This is true really even of such texts as *The Gospel in Solentiname,* by Ernesto Candnal. N.Y.: Orbis, 1976. Inevitably such accounts are selected & edited by the author of the book.

25. *Cf.* J.B. Metz in *Poverty of Spirit.* N.Y.: Paulist, 1968.

26. *Cf.* Lee Cormie, *op. cit.*

27. More especially by Julio de Santa Ana, *op. cit.* But *Cf.* also Cleage, *op. cit.,* and Nolan, *op. cit.*

28. *Cf.* the reference at the beginning of this essay to the Lonergan "organon" as descriptive of the proper method or program of theological work.

29. *E.g.,* in *An Essay in Aid of a Grammar of Assent.* N.Y.: Doubleday, 1955. (originally published in 1870 and reissued in 1978). Ch. 9, pp. 270-299.

30. *E.g.,* Gustavo Gutierrez, Enrique Dussel, Jon Sobrino, Ignacio Ellacuria, Hugo Assmann among others.

The Pere Marquette Theology Lectures

1969: "The Authority for Authority,"
by Quentin Quesnell
Professor of Theology at
Marquette University

1970: "Mystery and Truth,"
by John Macquarrie
Professor of Theology at
Union Theology Seminary, New York

1971: "Doctrinal Pluralism,"
by Bernard Lonergan, S.J.
Professor of Theology at
Regis College, Ontario

1972: "Infallibility,"
by George A. Lindbeck
Professor of Theology at
Yale University

1973: "Ambiguity in Moral Choice,"
by Richard A. McCormick, S.J.
Professor of Moral Theology at
Bellarmine School of Theology

1974: "Church Membership as a Catholic
and Ecumenical Problem,"
by Avery Dulles, S.J.
Professor of Theology at
Woodstock College

1975: "The Contributions of Theology to
Medical Ethics,"
by James Gustafson
University Professor of Theological Ethics at
University of Chicago

1976: "Religious Values in an Age of Violence,"
by Rabbi Marc Tanenbaum
Director of National Interreligious Affairs
American Jewish Committee, New York City

1977: "Truth Beyond Relativism: Karl Mannheim's
Sociology of Knowledge,"
by Gregory Baum
Professor of Theology and Religious Studies at
St. Michael's College

1978: "A Theology of 'Uncreated Energies'"
by George A. Maloney, S.J.
Professor of Theology
John XXIII Center For Eastern Christian Studies
Fordham University

1980: "Method in Theology: An Organon For
Our Time"
by Frederick E. Crowe, S.J.
Research Professor in Theology
Regis College, Toronto

1981: "Catholics in the Promised Land of
the Saints
by James Hennesey, S.J.
Professor of the History of Christianity
Boston College

1982: "Whose Experience Counts in
Theological Reflection?"
by Monika Hellwig
Professor of Theology at Georgetown
University

Copies of this lecture and the others in the series are
obtainable from:

Marquette University Press
Marquette University
Milwaukee, Wisconsin 53233
USA